Rookie
Poetry™
Holidays

let's celebrate

halloween

by J. Patrick Lewis

Children's Press®
An Imprint of Scholastic Inc.

Library of Congress Cataloging-in-Publication Data
A CIP catalog record for this book is available from the Library of Congress

Produced by Spooky Cheetah Press
Design by Anna Tunick Tabachnik (www.atunick.com)
Fonts: Coco Gothic, ITC Stone Informal
Clouds by freepik.com
Special thanks to Pamela Chanko for editorial advice

Printed in Heshan, China 62

SCHOLASTIC, CHILDREN'S PRESS, ROOKIE POETRY™, and associated logos are trademarks and/or registered trademarks of Scholastic Inc.

1 2 3 4 5 6 7 8 9 10 R 27 26 25 24 23 22 21 20 19 18

Photos ©: cover background: mythja/Shutterstock; cover bottom: holydude/iStockphoto; cover center: BilevichOlga/iStockphoto; cover bat and throughout: Terdpong/Shutterstock; back cover cupcakes: Rita Maas/Getty Images; back cover raven: Ilya D. Gridnev/Shutterstock; back cover cat silo: Cobalt Moon Design/Shutterstock; 1: mythja/Shutterstock; 2-3: Michael C. Gray/Shutterstock; 4 bottom right: Claude Charlebois/Getty Images; 5 main: quavondo/Getty Images; 5 jack-o-lanterns: Bernie DeChant/Getty Images; 5 center right pumpkin and throughout: Artshock/Dreamstime; 5 animal silos: Hein Nouwens/Shutterstock; 5 witch silo and throughout: N.Réka/Shutterstock; 5 center left branch silo: Olga Rom/Shutterstock; 5 gravestone silos: A-spring/Shutterstock; 5 tree silos: Ksanawo/Shutterstock; 5 bird silos: macrovector/iStockphoto; 5 cat silo and throughout: lalan/Shutterstock; 5 werewolf silo: blambca/Shutterstock; 6 bats and throughout: Portis Imaging/Alamy Images; 6 ghosts: Alexandra Grablewski/Getty Images; 6 bottom right: Klara Viskova/Shutterstock; 7 main: Hero/Media Bakery; 7 top skeletons: Colloidial/Dreamstime; 7 background: mythja/Shutterstock; 8-9 background: M_a_y_a/Getty Images; 8 grass: Sailorr/Shutterstock; 8 center: Alexandra Grablewski/Getty Images; 9 grass: Alhovik/Dreamstime; 9 bottom far left pumpkin: Leslie Banks/Dreamstime; 9 center: Catherine Delahaye/Getty Images; 9 bottom right: Franz-Marc Frei/Getty Images; 9 bottom center right pumpkin: AllaR15/Shutterstock; 9 bottom right pumpkins: Oldrich/Shutterstock; 9 bottom left pumpkin: RICIfoto/Shutterstock; 9 bottom center left pumpkin: Julia Tsokur/Shutterstock; 11 main: Jupiterimages/Getty Images; 11 center right face: Jupiterimages/Getty Images; 11 grass: Maxal Tamor/Shutterstock; 11 bat silos: YoPixArt/Shutterstock; 11 background: Michael C. Gray/Shutterstock; 12 bottom right candy: Kativ/Getty Images; 12 bottom right cupcake: Mary Ellen Bartley/Getty Images; 12-13 bottom: holydude/iStockphoto; 13 background sky: vovan13/iStockphoto; 13 main: Zing Images/Getty Images; 13 bat silos: Maglara/Shutterstock; 13 left bucket: Ariel Skelley/Getty Images; 13 center child: Nico Traut/Shutterstock; 14-15 lights: Kapitosh/Shutterstock; 14-15 candy: Hirkophoto/Getty Images; 14 apples: Foodcollection GesmbH/Getty Images; 14-15 candy: jenifoto/Getty Images; 15 left candy: GreenArtPhotography/iStockphoto; 15 center left candy: JeniFoto/Shutterstock; 15 center right candy: Walter B. McKenzie/Getty Images; 15 candy cauldron: CatLane/iStockphoto; 15 right cupcake: Mary Ellen Bartley/Getty Images; 16 cat: GK Hart/Vikki Hart/Getty Images; 16 top right and throughout: Reinke Fox/Shutterstock; 17 main: Colin Anderson/Getty Images; 17 ghosts: Lisa-Blue/Getty Images; 17 cape: Rido/Shutterstock; 17 skeleton: Burhan Bunardi/Shutterstock; 17 spider: IRCrockett/iStockphoto; 18 bottom right: Voinau Pavel/Shutterstock; 19 main: SDecha/Getty Images; 20 top left: Alexander Nicholson/Getty Images; 20 bottom left: NeydtStock/Shutterstock; 20 right: Richard Ellis/Getty Images; 21 top left: Michael Urban/Getty Images; 21 bottom left: Kees Metselaar/Alamy Images; 21 right: karambol/iStockphoto; 22 bottom left: Draga Saparevska Photografy/Getty Images; 23 top: Henry J. Ford/The Granger Collection; 23 center top: soloir/Getty Images; 23 center: Westend61/Getty Images; 23 center bottom: Catherine Delahaye/Getty Images; 23 bottom: quavondo/Getty Images.

Scholastic Inc., 557 Broadway, New York, NY 10012

table of contents

happy halloween!

Who rules the haunted castle there?
A king who's not a kidder.
The child who dares to cross his bridge
might want to **reconsider**.

FACT! There are more than 1,000 "haunted houses" in the U.S.

party time

It's Halloween! Let's have a party!
We'll paint our faces, wear long **gowns**,
bob for apples in a barrel,
carve up pumpkins, smiles
and frowns.

6

FACT!
Superhero
costumes are the
most popular
among kids.

how many teeth can a pumpkin have?

The pumpkin must have been
invented by a child
who thought the world could use
a vegetable that smiled.

8

guess who

Is that rabbit Angie Nicks
next to Leroy doing tricks?
Maybe Sam's the bumblebee?
Who's that scary skeleton? Me!

10

FACT! More than 41 million kids in the U.S. go trick-or-treating every year.

please give generously

Knock on the door, ring the bell,
wave your wand and cast a spell.
He's a robot, I'm a **hag**.
Won't you fill our candy bag?

FACT! Seven out of 10 Americans hand out candy on Halloween.

lots of pots of candy

I'll trade you red licorice for chocolate kisses,
or malted milk balls for the pick of the pot.
We'll snack for our supper on
trick-or-treat treasures.
Will Mom and Dad think it's okay?
Maybe not!

14

FACT! American kids eat about 3 pounds of candy each on Halloween.

dreams...
or nightmares?

Dream of witch, scratch an itch.

Dream of bat, scaredy cat.

Dream of ghost, you'll be toast.

Dream of mask...*do not ask!*

FACT!
Black cats
are a symbol
of Halloween
because they
are known as
witches' pets!

what's the good word?

What is the word that's used by witches, ghosts, and **goblins**—even you? That scary word you hear every October 31st is...*boo!*

FACT! Two of the most popular costumes for pets are pumpkin and hot dog.

spooky celebrations around the world

Ireland

Gotcha!
In Ireland, kids play a Halloween game called Snap Apple. They try to take a bite from an apple that is hanging from a string.

Mexico

France

March of the zombies
Limoges celebrates Halloween with a parade—of people dressed like ghosts and zombies.

Day of the Dead
People here believe their dead relatives come back to visit on Halloween. Many families decorate altars to their relatives with photos, flowers, and candy.

Germany

Great pumpkins

Every fall, Germany hosts the world's largest pumpkin fest. During the celebration, more than 400,000 pumpkins are turned into art.

Italy

Ghost party

In parts of Italy, many families set out a feast and then go to church. They leave the house open so their dead relatives can come in for a meal.

China

Feed the hungry

In southern China, Halloween is the Festival of the Hungry Ghosts. People believe ghosts roam the Earth. To ease the spirits, people burn food, fruit, or money.

halloween is...

...a time for spooky celebrations, ghosts, zombies, witches, and goblins! In the United States, we celebrate Halloween on October 31. This is the one day a year we can dress up as our favorite characters, go trick-or-treating, carve jack-o'-lanterns, and have fun at costume parties.

The holiday that became Halloween started more than 2,000 years ago in Great Britain. People believed that on October 31, spirits of the dead would return to Earth. The people wore masks when they went outside so they would look like spirits, too. Poor children practiced an early form of trick-or-treating. They would go door-to-door and sing or dance to receive food or money. Many years later, Irish immigrants brought this practice of trick-or-treating to America.

Over time, Halloween became the fun celebration we enjoy now!

glossary

goblins (GAH-blins): In fairy tales, goblins are small, ugly creatures who cause trouble.

gowns (GOUNS): Long dressses that are worn on special occasions.

hag (HAG): In fairy tales, a hag is a scary old woman who is mean to children.

invented (in-VENT-ed): Thought up and created something new.

reconsider (ree-kuhn-SID-ur): Think again about a previous decision, especially with the idea of making a change.

index

facts for now

Visit this Scholastic Web site to learn more about Halloween:
www.factsfornow.scholastic.com Enter the keyword **Halloween**

about the author

J. Patrick Lewis has published 100 children's picture and poetry
books to date with a wide variety of publishers. The Poetry
Foundation named him the third U.S. Children's Poet Laureate.